W9-AYQ-919

in
the
news™

THE ELECTION OF BARACK OBAMA

RACE AND POLITICS IN AMERICA

Jason Porterfield

ROSEN
PUBLISHING®
New York

Published in 2010 by The Rosen Publishing Group, Inc.
29 East 21st Street, New York, NY 10010

Copyright © 2010 by The Rosen Publishing Group, Inc.

First Edition

Library of Congress Cataloging-in-Publication Data

Porterfield, Jason.
The election of Barack Obama: race and politics in America / Jason Porterfield.
    p. cm. (In the news)
Includes bibliographical references and index.
ISBN 978-1-4358-3586-3 (library binding)
ISBN 978-1-4358-8554-7 (pbk)
ISBN 978-1-4358-8555-4 (6 pack)
1. Obama, Barack. 2. Presidents—United States—Election—2008.
3. Political campaigns—United States—History—21st century. 4. United States—Race relations. 5. United States—Politics and government—2001–
I. Title.
E907.P67 2010
973.932092—dc22

2009022968

5416
Manufactured in Malaysia

CPSIA Compliance Information: Batch #TWW10YA: For Further Information contact Rosen Publishing, New York, New York at 1-800-237-9932

On the cover: Clockwise from upper left: A large crowd gathers in Washington, D.C., to watch Barack Obama take the oath of office on January 20, 2009; a 1963 civil rights march in Washington, D.C.; Obama announces his plans to seek the Democratic Party's nomination for president at the Old State Capitol in Springfield, Illinois, in February 2007.

contents

Race and the Transformation of American Politics

Barack Obama's election as the forty-fourth president of the United States in 2008 marked a great shift in the way race is perceived in American politics. By defeating his opponent, Arizona Senator John McCain, Obama became the first African American to ever be elected president. The son of a white mother and a black father, he was viewed by many as a politician who could rise above old ideas about race and appeal to a broad range of voters.

Obama rose rapidly in politics. After spending a bit more than seven years as a state senator in Illinois, he was elected to the U.S. Senate in 2004. In 2008, Obama became the first African American to secure the presidential nomination of a major political party when voters chose him over New York Senator Hillary Clinton in a hotly contested primary battle. He took office on January 20, 2009.

In many ways, Obama's election victory was seen as a triumph over America's history of racial prejudice.

Barack Obama is sworn in as the forty-fourth president of the United States by Chief Justice John Roberts at the U.S. Capitol on January 20, 2009. Obama's wife, Michelle, and daughters, Malia *(left)* and Sasha *(right),* look on.

Obama won with the support of both African American and white voters. Three of the states that he won in the election—Florida, Virginia, and North Carolina—had seceded (left the country) at the beginning of the Civil War (1861–1865) and joined the Confederacy. Obama's victory in these states showed that ideas about race were changing, even in regions of the country that had once fought to preserve slavery.

Race and Diversity in the United States

The word "race" can mean many things to Americans. For some, race is defined by the color of a person's skin. Others define a person's race by his or her nationality. Still others may break a person's nationality into distinct ethnic groups, which may not share languages, religions, or customs.

According to the 2000 U.S. Census, about 75.1 percent of the U.S. population is white. Persons of Hispanic or Latino origin make up about 13 percent of the population, followed by African Americans, who make up 12.3 percent. About 3.6 percent of the population identifies as Asian American and 0.9 percent as Native American. Native Hawaiians or other Pacific Islander groups make up about 0.1 percent of the population. About 5.5 percent belong to some other race, and about 2.4 percent belong to more than one race.

The United States has often been described as a "melting pot" where immigrants from many nations and cultures come together and mix, creating a multicultural society. However, the country has had an uneasy history with diversity. Immigrants from around the world have faced prejudice and discrimination upon their arrival in the United States. They have often been treated as inferior by people whose families were already established in the country.

Discrimination based on race was not just common in the United States throughout the first half of the twentieth century—it was enforced by law. African Americans were often segregated from whites by "separate but equal" laws. These laws applied to public places ranging from movie theaters to schools. Segregation also extended to services such as public transportation, restrooms, and drinking fountains. In 1964, a law passed by Congress called the Civil Rights Act made segregation illegal. Congress passed another law in 1965 called the Voting Rights Act. This law made it illegal to deny any citizen the right to vote based on race.

Other racial and ethnic groups have also been treated poorly or excluded from the political process. For instance, Native Americans, whose cultures existed on the continent thousands of years before the first Europeans arrived in North America, suffered tremendously as European settlers pushed across the continent. In many cases, Native Americans were forcibly removed from their lands and sent to live on reservations.

During the second half of the twentieth century, the United States made great strides toward racial equality. Laws that had enforced racial discrimination were struck down. It became socially unacceptable for public figures—from politicians to celebrities—to make racist statements. Minorities have made great advances in politics, although the proportion of elected minority politicians is still much smaller than their percentage of the U.S. population.

The Tragedy of Slavery

The majority of early immigrants from Africa came to this country involuntarily. The first Africans were brought to Virginia as indentured servants in 1619. They had to work off the cost of their ocean voyage for a set number of years, after which they would be free. The transition from indentured servitude to slavery occurred gradually over the following decades. In 1662, Virginia's government passed a law stating that the children of black mothers would be classified as slaves or free citizens according to their mother's status.

Shortly after the Revolutionary War ended, many northern states made slavery illegal. In the southern states, the economy relied on massive plantations worked by slaves. Slavery was generally viewed as a necessary evil in these states. Slaveholders were allowed to treat their slaves as harshly as they wanted to. Politicians from the region further limited slaves' rights with restrictive laws. The treatment of slaves in the South initiated a pattern of oppression that would take centuries to overcome. By 1790, more than three hundred thousand slaves were living in the United States. These numbers grew rapidly, and by the time the Civil War began in 1861, the United States was home to an estimated four million slaves.

As time passed, the opponents of slavery became more vocal. These people, known as abolition-ists, were led by figures such as Henry Ward Beecher and Frederick Douglass, a former slave. In 1860, Abraham Lincoln, an opponent of slavery, was elected president of the United States. Following his

The abolitionist minister Henry Ward Beecher was an opponent of slavery in the United States before the Civil War. Beecher continued to advocate against racial discrimination after the war.

election, seven southern states seceded from the Union. Four other states seceded after the Civil War began in April 1861. These eleven states formed the

Confederate States of America, or the Confederacy. In 1862, Lincoln issued the Emancipation Proclamation, a document granting freedom to slaves.

The Civil War was a long and bloody battle. Ultimately, the Union Army defeated the Confederacy, in 1865. After the war, the country was reunited. Congress passed three amendments to the Constitution to protect the rights of the newly freed slaves. The Thirteenth Amendment ended slavery; the Fourteenth Amendment granted equal protection to all people; and the Fifteenth Amendment banned voting restrictions based on race.

Unfortunately, many white Americans resented the freedoms that were suddenly available to former slaves. Discriminatory laws and widespread racial prejudice made it very difficult for African American politicians to succeed during the late nineteenth and early twentieth centuries. This was particularly true in the South, where African Americans had historically been looked on as inferior in order to justify slavery. Throughout many parts of the country, state and local laws continued to limit the freedoms of African Americans.

Political Pioneers

In the decades following the Civil War, African Americans managed to make some headway in politics. At the time, the government was dominated by members of the Republican Party, which was led by politicians like Abraham Lincoln who wanted to limit or end slavery. They recognized that former African American slaves were strong supporters of their party. They believed that appointing qualified African Americans to political posts would help them maintain that support.

One such appointee was P. B. S. Pinchback, who was appointed governor of Louisiana in 1871 by President Ulysses S. Grant. Pinchback was the first African American governor of any state, and served out the final year of the previous governor's term. In fact, he remained the only African American governor in the United States until Virginia elected L. Douglas Wilder in 1989.

African Americans had successfully campaigned for political office in northern states before the Civil War. For example, in 1836, Vermont's Alexander Lucius Twilight became the first African American to be elected to a state legislature. Other African American politicians, such as John Mercer Langston of Ohio, served in local governments.

It would take until 1870 for an African American politician to be elected to the U.S. Congress. That year, voters in South Carolina elected Joseph Rainey to the House of Representatives. Other African Americans soon followed in Rainey's footsteps.

In the Senate, Hiram Revels (1827–1901) of Mississippi became the first African American senator in 1870, when the Mississippi State Legislature elected him to serve the remainder of a Senate term. In 1871, the Mississippi legislature again elected an African American to serve as a senator, sending Blanche Kelso Bruce (1841–1898) to Washington, D.C. Bruce was the last African American senator to serve until Edward Brooke of Massachusetts was elected in 1966. When Barack Obama was elected to serve in the Senate in 2004, he became only the fifth African American senator in the country's history and only the third to be elected by popular vote.

Several early African American politicians and statesmen are shown on this print, published in 1883. They include Frederick Douglass *(center)*, Blanche Kelso Bruce *(far upper right)*, P. B. S. Pinchback *(left)*, and John Mercer Langston *(lower left)*.

Race in the Twentieth Century

Barack Obama was born in Hawaii in 1961. He was raised by his mother and grandparents. His father, a native of Kenya, left the family to study at Harvard University in Massachusetts. During Obama's youth, the American civil rights movement was well underway. Minorities in the United States were working for equality. Growing up in Hawaii, Obama was relatively isolated from much of the racial strife that swept the country during the 1960s.

As Obama rose in the political ranks, he often acknowledged the importance of African Americans and other minority politicians who ran for office before him. Many of the African American politicians active during the second half of the twentieth century had close ties to the civil rights movement and worked to end segregation in American society. Younger African American politicians like Obama turned to these leaders for advice and support.

The Road to Freedom

Despite the passage of constitutional amendments after the Civil War that guaranteed the rights of African Americans, local laws continued to limit their ability to participate in government. African Americans were often unable to vote, as white politicians and poll workers devised strategies to keep them from casting votes. Some places, particularly in the South, required African Americans to pass difficult tests or pay expensive fees before they could vote. In other places, African Americans were kept away from the ballot box through intimidation and violence.

During the civil rights movement, leaders such as Martin Luther King Jr. encouraged people to engage in nonviolent protests against segregation. Many African Americans participated in these protests, which included marches and sit-ins. People who participated in sit-ins went into a segregated public space where African Americans were not allowed, such as a lunch counter. They remained in the public space until they were forcibly removed by the police. These actions helped bring about the Civil Rights Act of 1964, which outlawed racial segregation in schools, public places, and places of employment. Congress passed the Voting Rights Act, which ended discriminatory voting practices, in 1965.

Martin Luther King Jr. *(second from left)* leads a 1965 civil rights march in Alabama. Originating in the city of Selma, the march ended in the city of Montgomery. Such marches helped generate public support for the civil rights cause.

The civil rights movement brought about a significant political shift. The Democratic Party, which had tolerated and even advocated racial discrimination since the Civil War, shifted to become a more liberal party as President Lyndon B. Johnson threw his support behind the civil rights movement. The Republican Party became more conservative and actively resisted the civil rights movement. Some Democrats—particularly in the South, where opposition to the civil rights movement was high—crossed over to the Republican Party. Others supported candidates who ran campaigns in open opposition to the civil rights movement, such as Governor George Wallace of Alabama.

A New Generation of Politicians

The civil rights movement helped usher in a new generation of African American politicians. One of these politicians was Edward W. Brooke, a liberal Republican from Massachusetts. In 1949, Brooke first ran for office in Massachusetts, where he lost a race for a seat in the state's House of Representatives. He then ran for office two more times and was finally elected as Massachusetts' attorney general in 1962. In 1966, he became the first African American to be elected senator since the nineteenth century. Brooke would serve in the Senate until 1979.

In 1967, President Lyndon B. Johnson nominated Thurgood Marshall to serve as a justice on the U.S. Supreme Court. Marshall was the first African American ever nominated for this position. He had first made a name for himself as a lawyer arguing civil rights cases. Marshall was easily confirmed by the Senate and served as a justice until 1991. He was replaced on the bench by Clarence Thomas, another African American.

Shirley Chisholm's Pioneering Run

Obama was the first African American elected president, but he was not the first to run for the office. U.S.

In 1972, U.S. Representative Shirley Chisholm became the first African American to run for a major political party's presidential nomination.

Representative Shirley Chisholm (1924–2005) declared her candidacy for the Democratic Party's nomination in the 1972 presidential election. This made Chisholm the first African American to campaign for a major political party's presidential nomination. She was a relative newcomer to politics. A former teacher, Chisholm was first elected to a political office in 1964, when she won a seat in the New York General Assembly. She served there during the height of the civil rights movement.

Chisholm became the first African American woman to serve in Congress after being elected to a vacant seat, in 1968. There, she became an outspoken critic of the Vietnam War (1959–1975) and an advocate for civil rights and equality for women. She spoke not just for African Americans, but also for other minorities. Chisholm referred to herself as "unbought and unbossed," and sometimes clashed with other members of the

Congressional Black Caucus—a group of African American lawmakers in Congress who focused on social issues—over her political views.

When Chisholm decided to run for the presidential nomination, she faced several well-seasoned politicians. Among them were former vice president Hubert Humphrey, who had won the party's nomination in 1968, only to lose the election to Republican Richard Nixon; and Senator George McGovern, who went on to win the nomination.

Though she did not win the party's nomination, Chisholm won primary elections in Louisiana and Mississippi, two states with large African American populations. She ended up winning about 10 percent of the votes cast in the primary. Chisholm returned to Congress after the convention and served until her retirement in 1982.

Jesse Jackson's Rainbow Coalition

An influential African American religious leader and politician, the Reverend Jesse Jackson was a prominent figure during the civil rights movement. Jackson sought the Democratic Party's presidential nomination in 1984 and 1988.

Jackson was active in many social causes before announcing that he would run for the 1984 Democratic

Party nomination. In both of his presidential campaigns, Jackson sought to include numerous minority groups in what he called a "rainbow coalition." Jackson sought to capture the support not only of African Americans, but also Hispanic Americans, Asian Americans, Arab Americans, Native Americans, as well as broader social classes like family farmers, working-class Americans, and white progressives.

Jackson made a strong showing in 1984, winning five primaries and caucuses. He captured 3,282,431 primary votes, or 18.2 percent of the total. He finished third behind eventual nominee Vice President Walter Mondale and Senator Gary Hart.

In many ways, Jackson was a controversial candidate. Ironically, his chances of winning in 1984 were hurt by racially insensitive remarks that he had made about Jewish people during an interview that January. Jackson apologized for his remarks, but the controversy created a rift between Jackson and the Jewish community.

This controversy did not stop Jackson from running again in 1988. His strong showing in 1984 convinced many that he was a serious candidate, and he ended up winning seven primaries and four caucuses. He captured 6.9 million votes and was briefly considered the front-runner for the nomination. However, a

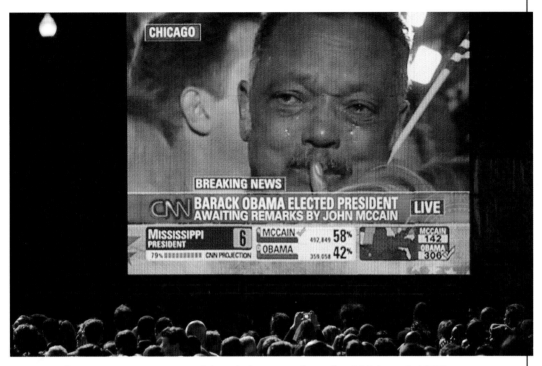

Jesse Jackson ran strong presidential campaigns in 1984 and 1988. Here, he is shown at a rally for Barack Obama in Chicago, reacting to the announcement that Obama had won the 2008 presidential election.

decisive loss in the Wisconsin primary helped seal the presidential nomination for Massachusetts Governor Michael Dukakis.

Though Jackson did not run for president again after 1988, he remained politically influential. In 1990, he was elected as a "shadow senator" for Washington, D.C., an unofficial office that lobbies for the city's right to full representation in Congress. Jackson held this position until 1997. He remained an influential figure in American politics. Candidates continued to seek Jackson's support into the 2008 presidential election.

Governor L. Douglas Wilder

When Virginia Governor L. Douglas Wilder declared that he would run for the 1992 Democratic presidential nomination, he was a little-known figure in American politics. However, Wilder had accomplished the feat of becoming just the second African American governor in U.S. history and the first African American to be elected to the position.

Wilder's political rise was a slow one, however. He was elected to the Virginia Senate in 1969 and held the seat until 1985, when he decided to run for the state's attorney general position. Wilder knew that he would have to find a way to appeal to white voters in a state where segregation had ended just twenty years before. He spent two months campaigning throughout the state's rural areas, introducing himself to voters. The campaign paid off, and Wilder became the first statewide African American elected official in Virginia's history.

Wilder built on his win, announcing that he would run for governor in 1989. The popular Wilder had little trouble securing the Democratic nomination. He faced former Virginia attorney general Marshall Coleman, a Republican, in the governor's race. Wilder won what turned out to be a very close race, becoming Virginia's first elected African American governor.

Because of Virginia's term limits, Wilder served just one term as governor. In 1991, he announced that he would run for president. His campaign, however, attracted little support. Wilder dropped out of the race before the primaries began. He returned to politics in 2004 and was elected mayor of Richmond, Virginia.

Colin Powell

General Colin Powell was a career soldier who served as the first African American chairman of the U.S. Army's Joint Chiefs of Staff from 1989 to 1993. Serving under President George H. W. Bush, Powell became the public face of the army during the first Gulf War (1990–1991). Powell was widely respected by many politicians.

When Powell retired from the military in 1993, many anticipated that he would seek the Republican presidential nomination in 1996. He had been mentioned as a possible running mate for President George H. W. Bush's reelection bid in 1992.

Powell declared himself a Republican in 1995 and began campaigning for Republican candidates. Many saw this move as a step toward launching his own presidential campaign for the 1996 election. Some polls taken at the time showed that Powell could win the

General Colin Powell was seen as a potential presidential candidate before the 1996 election. Powell, a Republican, endorsed Obama in 2008.

election against President Bill Clinton. Ultimately, Powell declined to run for president, but not before awakening many Americans to the possibility of voting for an African American candidate.

In 2001, Powell became the first African American secretary of state. He was appointed to that position by President George W. Bush. Powell resigned as secretary of state in 2005 and was replaced by another African American, Condoleezza Rice.

Carol Moseley Braun and Al Sharpton

The 2004 presidential election marked the first time in U.S. history that two prominent African American figures ran for the Democratic nomination. Carol Moseley Braun was a senator from Illinois from 1993 to 1999 and had been the first African American woman elected to the Senate. After losing a reelection bid, she served as an ambassador to New Zealand from 1999 to 2001. Her 2004 campaign marked the second time that an African American woman ran for president.

The Reverend Al Sharpton was an activist during the civil rights movement and frequently spoke out on controversial social justice issues in the years that followed. Sharpton ran unsuccessfully for a U.S. Senate seat in 1988, 1992, and 1994, failing to capture the Democratic nomination each time. Sharpton also ran unsuccessfully for mayor of New York City in 1997.

Moseley Braun and Sharpton were just two candidates in a crowded race, and neither candidate attracted much support. Moseley Braun dropped out before the first caucus. Sharpton hung on until March, when he left the race and endorsed eventual nominee John Kerry.

Obama's Rise

I n his 1995 memoir, *Dreams from My Father*, Barack Obama recalls feeling as though he was living in two different worlds, one white and one black. He talks about growing up in a multicultural environment in Hawaii and—from age six to age ten—Indonesia.

When he left Hawaii in 1979 to attend Occidental College in Los Angeles, Obama experienced culture shock. In Hawaii, he felt that many cultures blended together in a tolerant atmosphere. In Los Angeles, things were different. Obama became active in African American organizations in college, especially after transferring to Columbia University in New York City, in 1981. He graduated from there in 1983 with a degree in sociology.

He left New York in 1985, moving to Chicago to take a job as a community organizer for a church-based nonprofit group called the Developing Communities Project. As the group's director, he worked in low-income, predominantly African American communities on Chicago's South Side. Obama helped establish a job training program, a tutoring program, and a tenant's rights organization for residents of one of the city's public housing developments.

He left Chicago in 1988 to attend Harvard Law School. During his first year there, Obama served as editor of the school's *Harvard Law Bulletin*. In his second year, Obama became the first African American elected as the magazine's president. He graduated magna cum laude in 1991.

The Obamas' Early Involvement in Politics

Obama returned to Chicago after earning his law degree. In 1992, he directed a voter registration drive called Project Vote. With a staff of ten full-time workers and seven hundred volunteers, Obama succeeded in registering 150,000 African American voters in Illinois. That year, he also began teaching constitutional law at the University of Chicago Law School and worked as an attorney specializing in civil rights cases.

Obama also married Michelle Robinson that year. Robinson grew up in Chicago, where her father worked for the city's water department and her mother was a secretary. She graduated from Princeton University and earned a law degree from Harvard Law School in 1988. She met her future husband while they were both working as attorneys for the same Chicago law firm.

Barack Obama is shown here working in Chicago on a voter registration drive in 1992. Obama returned to Chicago shortly after graduating from Harvard Law School in 1991.

After their marriage, Michelle Obama went to work in administrative roles for the city of Chicago. She also worked for the University of Chicago, serving as the associate dean of student services, and as vice president for community and external affairs for the University of Chicago Hospitals.

The Illinois Senate

In 1995, Barack Obama decided to run as a Democrat for an open Senate seat in Illinois' thirteenth district. The seat had been held by another African American Democrat, Alice Palmer. Palmer had announced that she planned to give up the seat in order to run for a vacant congressional seat in a special election. At the time, the district covered many of the African American communities that Obama had served when he worked for the Developing Communities Project. He won the seat easily, capturing 82 percent of the vote. Obama served three terms in the Illinois Senate, winning reelection bids in 1998 and 2002.

An Early Defeat

In 1999, he announced that he would challenge U.S. Representative Bobby Rush in the 2000 Democratic primary. While Obama was a relative newcomer, Rush was an established African American politician with deep roots in Chicago. He had represented his district since 1993. Before that, he served as an alderman on Chicago's City Council during the tenure of Mayor Harold Washington, the city's first African American mayor. In the late 1960s, Rush had also been a founder of the Illinois chapter of the radical Black Panther Party, a political organization that advocated both social involvement and militant self-defense for African American communities.

During the campaign, Rush said that Obama's roots in Chicago's black communities were not deep enough for him to represent the district, which was 65 percent African American. Rush also emphasized his own experiences during the civil rights era. While he avoided using racial terms directly, Rush succeeded in turning Obama's background against him. He painted Obama as an elitist who had come from a privileged background and mocked him for his Harvard education. Obama replied that he could help bridge the gap between whites and African Americans, but to no avail. Many of Illinois' African American leaders in the Democratic Party came out in support of Rush instead of Obama. Obama lost the primary election, getting only 31 percent of the vote.

The Race for the Senate

Obama was disappointed by the outcome of the congressional race, but he continued serving his constituents in the Illinois Senate. He made amends with African American leaders who had supported Rush and became known for his ability to work with Republican lawmakers. As Obama gained more influence, he was able to write and pass more legislation.

In 2003, Obama announced that he would run for the U.S. Senate seat once held by Carol Moseley Braun. He secured his party's nomination in the Democratic

The 2004 Illinois senate race between Barack Obama and Alan Keyes marked the first time that two African Americans were the major party nominees in a U.S. Senate election.

primary, winning 53 percent of the vote in an unexpected landslide against six other candidates. Early polls showed him ahead of all eight possible Republican nominees. Obama's numbers improved further when the eventual Republican nominee, Jack Ryan, withdrew from the race because of a scandal.

Ryan's withdrawal forced the Republicans to find a new nominee. They settled on Alan Keyes, a conservative African American activist and former diplomat from

Maryland. Keyes had run unsuccessfully for the U.S. Senate in 1988 and 1992, and had also launched failed attempts for the Republican presidential nomination in 1996 and 2000. His status as a nationally known political figure did not help him in the race. Keyes had never lived in Illinois, and many residents saw him as an outsider.

During the weeks before Keyes entered the race, Obama followed the example of former Virginia governor L. Douglas Wilder and toured heavily in rural parts of Illinois in an effort to get to know residents. The strategy worked, and Obama won with 70 percent of the vote. Keyes only won 27 percent of the vote. It was the largest margin of victory for a statewide race in Illinois history.

Media Attention

The race for the Democratic Party's nomination brought national attention to Barack Obama. His strong victory in the primary made him a rising star in the Democratic Party, and he was invited to give the keynote address at the 2004 Democratic National Convention.

In his speech, Obama spoke of the need for Americans to overcome their differences. "There is not a black America and a white America and Latino America and Asian America—there's the United States of America," he told the crowd. He emphasized his interracial background, his upbringing in Hawaii and Indonesia, and how lucky he was to have the opportunity to attend Harvard, even though he did not come from a wealthy family. To conclude the speech, he emphasized the power of hope, and referred to his younger self as "a skinny kid with a funny name who believes that America has a place for him, too."

The speech, which was viewed or heard by millions of Americans, made Obama an overnight sensation. Figures in the media began discussing the possibility of a presidential run in Obama's future. It appeared that Obama's emphasis on his diverse background helped him

Barack Obama's famous keynote address to delegates at the 2004 Democratic National Convention is often credited with helping him become a major star within the party.

identify with a wide range of people. The speech was also seen as signaling a transition in African American political leadership.

Securing the Nomination

O n a cold February morning in 2007, Senator Barack Obama addressed a crowd in Springfield, the state capital of Illinois. Standing in front of the Old State Capitol and speaking just two days before Abraham Lincoln's birthday, Obama evoked Lincoln's memory as he declared the he was entering the 2008 race for president of the United States. Obama referenced Lincoln's famous statement that "a house divided cannot stand" and declared that, as president, he would work to build a brighter future.

Building Momentum

Speculation about a possible presidential run for Obama had built since he took office as a senator, even though he had told reporters after his victory that he would not run in 2008. As the rising star of the Democratic Party, he made numerous appearances on behalf of candidates

Obama announced his run for the Democratic presidential nomination in Springfield, Illinois, at the site of Abraham Lincoln's famous "A House Divided" speech.

running in the 2006 election. Among the candidates he campaigned for were Deval Patrick, an African American attorney and the Democratic nominee in Massachusetts' gubernatorial election. Patrick went on to win the four-way race with 56 percent of the vote, becoming the second African American elected governor.

Obama also appeared with Harold Ford Jr., an African American Congressman who was running for an open Senate seat in Tennessee. Ford was a member of a politically prominent family in Tennessee and had given the keynote address at the 2000 Democratic National Convention. If elected, Ford would be the first African American senator from the South since the nineteenth century. However, he was locked in a tight race for the Senate seat with the Republican nominee, former Chattanooga mayor Bob Corker.

Late in the campaign, the Republican National Committee (the fund-raising and organizational arm of the Republican Party) ran an anti-Ford television commercial that many saw as racially charged. The commercial featured a scantily clad white actress—supposedly portraying a woman who had met Ford at a Super Bowl party—asking Ford to call her. The National Association for the Advancement of Colored People (NAACP), an African American advocacy group, charged that the commercial played on old racist fears about interracial dating.

Both candidates condemned the commercial, and Corker's campaign asked the party to stop running the ad. Ford ultimately lost the election by a narrow margin, and some analysts believed that the commercial had an impact. The controversy over the advertisement showed that, even forty years after the civil rights movement, race could still be a divisive factor in a political campaign.

The Democrats did not have a monopoly on African American candidates in the 2006 election. Lynn Swann and Ken Blackwell were the Republican nominees for governor in Pennsylvania and Ohio, respectively, while Michael Steele was the party's nominee for an open Senate seat in Maryland. None of these Republican candidates won, though Steele went on to become the first African American head of the Republican Party in 2009. The Republican Party was more successful in running a minority candidate in 2007, when Indian American candidate Bobby Jindal won a four-way race to become governor of Louisiana.

Launching the Obama Campaign

When Barack Obama announced in 2007 that he was entering the race for the Democratic presidential nomination, the front-runner for the nomination was New York Senator Hillary Rodham Clinton. Clinton had also been first lady from 1993 to 2001, during the presidency of her husband, Bill Clinton. She won an election for an open U.S. Senate seat in New York in 2000 and was reelected in 2006. Clinton had been preparing for a presidential bid for years, and was running far ahead of Obama and the other candidates through most of 2007.

Apart from Clinton and Obama, the field for the nomination included six candidates. Among them were former North Carolina senator John Edwards, who was

Democratic hopefuls stand with Chairman of the Democratic National Committee Howard Dean before a 2008 presidential debate. Pictured are *(left to right)* Chris Dodd, Joe Biden, John Edwards, Hillary Clinton, Howard Dean, Barack Obama, Dennis Kucinich, and Bill Richardson.

the 2004 nominee for vice president; New Mexico Governor Bill Richardson; Delaware Senator Joe Biden; Connecticut Senator Chris Dodd; former Alaska senator Mike Gravel; and Ohio Representative Dennis Kucinich. Clinton, Obama, and Edwards quickly became the front-runners in the race.

Obama attracted a great deal of praise when he entered the race, but he also generated some negative attention. Early in the race, fellow candidate Joe Biden caused an uproar when he referred to Obama as "the first mainstream African American who is articulate and bright and clean and a nice-looking guy." Some critics saw the remarks as a slight against past African American candidates. Biden later apologized for the remarks and insisted that no slight was intended.

In May 2007, the U.S. Secret Service, the agency that provides security for presidential candidates as well as for the president of the United States, announced that it would begin providing security for Obama. It marked the earliest point in a presidential campaign that a candidate had been offered security protection. The agency indicated that the move was necessary because a high number of threats had been made against Obama.

The Primary Season

Clinton maintained her lead in the polls through late 2007, when Obama began gaining ground. He finished ahead of the other candidates in the Iowa caucus, the first race of the primary season, with 38 percent of the vote. Edwards finished second, and Clinton finished third. This was seen as a significant win for Obama because it showed that he could win in a state with a large white majority.

During the primary campaign, Obama occasionally faced criticism from the African American community. Some African Americans felt that Obama's Ivy League education, as well as the fact that he was raised by a white mother and grandparents, isolated him from the experiences of the majority of African Americans. Obama largely dismissed these criticisms.

Obama quickly lost momentum, however, when Clinton won the next primary, held in New Hampshire. Despite the fact that some polls taken before the primary had put Obama ahead of Clinton by ten or more percentage points, Clinton won by three points.

The Bradley Effect

After New Hampshire, some Obama supporters became worried about a controversial political phenomenon called the Bradley effect. The Bradley effect was named for former Los Angeles mayor David Bradley. Mayor Bradley, an African American, lost the 1982 governor's race in California despite leading in voter polls before the election. The theory behind the Bradley effect is that some white voters may tell poll takers that they plan to vote for an African American candidate but instead support another candidate or end up not voting.

The phenomenon also occurred during L. Douglas Wilder's run for governor of Virginia, in 1989. Wilder led his opponent in polls taken just before the election, but ended up winning by less than 1 percent of the vote.

Some analysts argued that the Republicans made a strong effort to bring voters to the polls, while Democratic voters may have felt complacent about the election, believing that Wilder could not lose. Others, citing the Bradley effect, stated that some white voters might have indicated that they would support Wilder, despite having no intention of doing so, in order not to appear racist. The New Hampshire primary was the first point in the Obama campaign that the Bradley effect seemed a real possibility.

Race also came to the foreground as the candidates started campaigning before the South Carolina primary, the first primary of the season to feature a large African American voting block. By then, the field had narrowed to Obama, Clinton, and Edwards. While Hillary Clinton campaigned in some states where she was running behind, Bill Clinton went on a speaking tour through the state. During his own presidential campaigns, Bill Clinton had always been very popular with African American voters. However, he alienated many African American voters by comparing Obama's projected win in the primary with Jesse Jackson's in 1988 and painting Obama as "the black candidate." Obama ended up winning the primary with 55 percent of the vote. Hillary Clinton finished a distant second, with 27 percent, while Edwards captured only 18 percent of the vote.

The Jeremiah Wright Controversy

Obama and Clinton remained in a very tight race as they entered the March primaries. That month, videos of Obama's pastor at the time, the Reverend Jeremiah Wright, began receiving media attention. Wright, an African American, was the head of a Chicago church that Obama had attended since 1988. Obama had highly praised Wright in speeches and in his writing, citing his pastor's dedication to the church and to his community.

Wright was also a product of the civil rights movement, and founded his church on the principles of a religious movement called black liberation theology. Black liberation theology maintains that African Americans must use the teachings of Jesus Christ to free themselves from social, economic, political, and religious bondage.

Wright became a problem for the Obama campaign when video of some of his speeches became public. In the speeches, Wright used strong language to criticize American society. Media commentators began questioning Obama's judgment in choosing to attend Wright's church.

Shortly after the controversy began, Obama addressed the topic of race in a speech given in Philadelphia. The speech, titled "A More Perfect Union," addressed issues of anger on the part of African Americans, and resentment on the part of whites, in an attempt to give context to some of Wright's remarks. Obama condemned the language Wright used but did not criticize the pastor himself. Instead, he spoke again of his biracial background and urged the nation to move beyond the issue of race and begin addressing the social problems shared by all. Obama later left the church in order to avoid becoming a distraction to the congregation.

The speech was heard by millions of Americans and was widely praised by politicians and commentators. Instead of allowing the controversy over Wright to damage his campaign, Obama had used the opportunity to speak candidly to the public about race.

Barack Obama stands with his family on August 28, 2008, in Denver, Colorado, after accepting the Democratic Party's presidential nomination.

Clinton and Obama remained locked in their primary race until late May, when Obama took a commanding lead. Clinton finally left the race in early June, making Obama the Democratic nominee. The party made his nomination official at the 2008 Democratic National Convention, held in Denver in August.

The Presidential Campaign

5

At the end of the primary season, Barack Obama
stood as the first African American major party
candidate in the history of the United States.
He would face the Republican Party nominee, Arizona
Senator John McCain, in the presidential election in
November.

The presidential campaign was the second of
McCain's career. He also ran for the Republican nomination in 2000, only to lose to George W. Bush, who went
on to win the election that year. A decorated veteran
known for having an independent streak and an ability
to cross party lines, McCain had a brief surge early in
the 2000 campaign but dropped out after losing to Bush
in the South Carolina primary.

Many thought that McCain would win the Republican
Party's presidential nominee in the 2000 campaign. After
McCain lost the nomination, his supporters charged
that Bush supporters had stirred up racial tensions to
derail McCain's campaign. McCain and his wife, Cindy,

who are white, have a dark-skinned adopted daughter of Bangladeshi descent. Anonymous poll takers played on racial prejudices by spreading rumors that the daughter was actually McCain's own illegitimate African American daughter.

Republican candidate John McCain and Barack Obama face each other during a 2008 presidential debate.

Taking the Focus Off of Race

The issue of race remains sensitive in many parts of the country, and in many cases old prejudices are closer to the surface than many Americans may realize. In South Carolina, memories of the Civil War and the civil rights movement remain very fresh. In recent years, the NAACP has even initiated a travel boycott of South Carolina because the state has refused to take down a Confederate battle flag that has flown on the grounds of the State House since 1962. The flag was removed from the roof of the State House in 2000, but still flies prominently over a memorial to the state's Confederate war dead.

Both McCain and Obama largely refrained from making race an issue in the 2008 campaign. Obama had spent the Democratic primary working to cast himself as not just an African American candidate but as one who represented all Americans. McCain consciously avoided the issue of race in his campaign and rejected strategies and endorsements that could be seen as racially charged. For example, despite advice from people within his own campaign, he refused to try to use the Reverend Jeremiah Wright's speeches against Obama.

Debunking Rumors

Many people opposed to Obama's campaign believed that McCain and the Republican Party should use every weapon available against the Democratic nominee, including unfounded rumors about Obama's personal history. Media commentators attacked Obama's background and religion on television and radio, as well as in print. The people spreading these rumors hoped to convince undecided white voters that Obama was untrustworthy because he might not share their background. These rumors date back to his run for the U.S. Senate in 2004, though they received little media coverage at the time.

The most persistent of these rumors questioned Obama's religion and nationality. These rumors were largely built around the faith and nationality of Obama's

In her village in Kenya, Barack Obama's grandmother Sarah Obama holds up photos of his wedding to Michelle and his late father. Some of Obama's opponents questioned his nationality based on his Kenyan heritage.

father, also named Barack Obama. Obama's father was born a Muslim in Kenya, though he lost interest in religion at a young age and became an atheist. He and Obama's mother, Ann Dunham, divorced in 1964. Obama's father returned to Kenya, where he lived until his death in 1982.

Some of the rumors spread against Obama alleged that he is not eligible to serve as president because he was not born in the United States. The Constitution of the United States declares that someone who wasn't born in the United States cannot be elected president. One of these rumors alleged that Obama was actually born in Kenya, rather than in Hawaii. Other rumors claimed that he is a dual citizen of the United States and Kenya, or that he became a citizen of Indonesia when he lived there briefly as a child.

The rumors about Obama's citizenship persisted, even after the Hawaii state government issued a copy of

Obama's birth certificate. Obama's birth certificate clearly shows that he was born in Hawaii. Critics charged that the document was a fake and demanded that Obama publicly release his personal copy of his birth certificate. Obama has ignored these demands. The rumors even led to some court cases, in which people have sued to get the courts to block Obama from taking office. So far, three such suits have been filed with the U.S. Supreme Court, though the court has judged that these cases have no merit and has refused to hear them.

Other rumors have claimed that Obama is secretly a Muslim. Prejudice against Muslims increased in the United States after the September 11, 2001, terrorist attacks on the World Trade Center and the Pentagon, which were carried out by Muslim extremists. Some media commentators and religious leaders have often added to these sentiments through statements attacking Islam and Muslims.

The rumors that Obama is a Muslim stem from his father's upbringing, as well as the fact that he has relatives in Kenya who are practicing Muslims. Rumors also referenced Obama's middle name, Hussein, which was given to Obama in honor of his grandfather. During the presidential campaign, conservative commentators and politicians often made a point of using Obama's middle name in an attempt to build associations between Obama and the former Iraqi dictator Saddam Hussein in the minds of voters.

Some rumors have even claimed that Obama attended an Islamic religious school while living in Indonesia, even though his attendance at two secular schools is well documented. Obama referenced his Christian faith many times during his campaign. His own membership in the congregation of Trinity United Church of Christ was easily proven and became very public during the Jeremiah Wright controversy.

Though it had no basis in fact, this rumor played on fears that Obama was different from the average "mainstream" American citizen. Religion often plays a major roll in political campaigns, particularly for Americans with conservative political beliefs. Since the nation's founding, no member of a specifically non-Christian religion has been elected president.

Rather than let the rumors become a distraction, the Obama campaign adopted a policy of debunking them as soon as they appeared. The strategy worked, and the rumors ended up having little effect on the campaign.

Winning the Election

Obama's campaign was well-organized and well-funded. His opponent belonged to the same political party as President George W. Bush, who had a very low popularity rating. In addition, McCain had supported many of Bush's policies. Obama had proved that he was able to

Volunteers for the Obama campaign worked hard to spread the message about their candidate. The Obama campaign built a massive network of enthusiastic volunteers, particularly among young people.

cross racial lines and draw support from white voters as well as from minority voters. Polls taken just before the election showed that Obama and his running mate, Senator Joe Biden, would win the election by a comfortable margin. They ended up winning with 69,498,215 votes—or 52.9 percent of the popular vote—and 365 electoral votes. John McCain and his running mate, Alaska Governor Sarah Palin, finished with 59,948,240 votes, or 45.7 percent of the popular vote, and 173 electoral votes. Obama won twenty-eight states to McCain's twenty-two. As major news networks called the election in Obama's favor, celebrations broke out across the country.

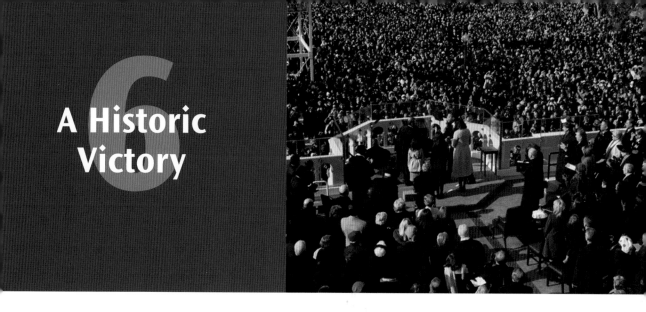

A Historic Victory

6

Barack Obama took office as the forty-fourth president of the United States on January 20, 2009, to much fanfare. More than two million people traveled to Washington, D.C., to witness this historic event. People expressed hope and optimism that the Obama presidency would help bring forth a new era of race relations in the United States.

Breaking Down the Vote

Obama won the popular election by nearly ten million votes across the country. About 95 percent of voters identifying themselves as African American voted for him, as did 67 percent of Hispanics. Obama lost among white voters—43 percent of whom supported him—but actually performed better than 2004 Democratic Party nominee John Kerry, who drew just 40 percent of the white vote. Among Obama's supporters, 61 percent

The swearing-in of the nation's first African American president generated excitement around the world. People flocked to D.C. for the inauguration.

were white, 23 percent were African American, and 11 percent were Hispanic.

Significantly, for the first time in U.S. presidential election history, fewer than 75 percent of voters were white. About 74 percent of voters identified themselves as white, 13 percent as African American, and 11 percent as Hispanic. The remaining 2 percent of voters identified themselves as belonging to more than one race. The percentage of voters identifying themselves as African American was an all-time high.

Only 19 percent of voters said that race was a factor for them in the 2008 presidential election. Among these voters, Obama won by a margin of 53 percent to 47 percent. Among white voters, 17 percent said that race was a factor. Of those voters, only 37 percent voted for Obama, compared to 61 percent for McCain. One in three African American voters said that race was a factor. Those voters overwhelmingly supported Obama.

The Roland Burris Controversy

One outcome of Obama's election was a possible change in the makeup of the Senate. In the country's history, only 125 African Americans have served in Congress. Of that number, five—including Obama—were senators.

As a U.S. senator from Illinois, Barack Obama was the only African American serving in the Senate when he was elected president. He resigned his Senate seat on November 16, 2008. Under Illinois law, the governor has the power to appoint a successor to fill out the remainder of a senate term. Pressure was put on Illinois governor Rod Blagojevich to appoint an African American to take Obama's place. Blagojevich, however, drew out the process until he was arrested on federal charges of trying to profit from the appointment.

After his arrest, Blagojevich was pressured to allow the Illinois General Assembly to choose a successor so that the new senator would not be tainted by connections to the governor. Blagojevich instead appointed Roland Burris to Obama's Senate seat. Burris, an African American, was a longtime Illinois politician who had served as the

Judge Judith W. Rogers *(right)* from the U.S. Court of Appeals of the District of Columbia administers the ceremonial oath of office to the Congressional Black Caucus in January 2009.

state's attorney general from 1991 to 1995.

The appointment of Burris caused a controversy throughout the state and in Congress. Some politicians refused to accept the appointment, while others—including the Congressional Black Caucus—demanded that Burris be allowed to take the seat. Burris's opponents relented, and Burris was sworn in as the sixth African American senator in the nation's history.

Forty-two African Americans now serve in Congress, including Burris and two nonvoting delegates representing U.S. territories. There are two African American governors, Deval Patrick of Massachusetts and David Paterson of New York. Paterson took office in 2008 after former governor Eliot Spitzer resigned.

The First One Hundred Days

Race was not a major issue on Obama's agenda early in his administration. He began his term by concentrating on issues such as the economy and the wars in Iraq and Afghanistan. In February 2009, U.S. Attorney General Eric Holder, an African American who had been appointed by Obama, called the United States "a nation of cowards" in terms of discussing race.

Holder had hoped to start a national dialogue on race, but the remarks set off a controversy in the media as commentators either praised him or condemned his remarks. Obama later said that he believes the country should do more to face up to its legacy of slavery and discrimination. However, he also distanced himself from the remarks, saying that he didn't believe that constantly talking about race would help solve racial tensions. The response upset some African American leaders, who have criticized Obama for de-emphasizing race since his term began.

However, Americans in general remain optimistic about Obama's presidency. A poll conducted in April 2009 by the New York Times and CBS News showed that about 66 percent of Americans believe that race relations in the United States are "good," up from 53 percent in July 2008. Among African Americans polled, 70 percent said that the country was headed in the right direction, and 72 percent of all Americans polled said that they felt optimistic about the next four years.

Glossary

advocate A supporter of a person or a cause.

alderman A member of a municipal legislative body, such as a city council.

amendment An addition or change made to a document, such as a constitution, bill, statute, or motion.

campaign The race between candidates for public office before an election.

constituent A citizen who is represented in government by an elected official.

constitution A document that embodies the fundamental principles and laws of a nation, state, or other political or social organization.

controversy A public dispute between sides holding differing opinions.

discrimination A difference in treatment based on factors other than merit, such as race or gender.

diversity A variety, as of different forms or qualities.

ethnic Pertaining to a group of people with a common culture, religion, race, language, or national origin.

immigrant A person who enters and settles in a foreign country or region.

indentured servant A person who agrees to work for another for a specified period of time in return for passage to a new country or instruction in a trade.

intimidation The use of threats to coerce a person or group of people to do something.

magna cum laude A Latin phrase meaning "with great praise." It is an honor given to graduates to denote special academic achievement.

nomination The act of officially naming a candidate for an election.

poll A sampling or collection of opinions on a subject.

prejudice Unreasonable dislike or suspicion of a particular racial, religious, or national group.

primary An election in which voters of a particular political party nominate candidates.

reservation A tract of land set aside for use by Native American tribes.

secular Not connected to or relating to religion.

segregate To separate by race, religion, or any other quality.

For More Information

Congressional Black Caucus Foundation

1720 Massachusetts Avenue NW

Washington, DC 20036

(202) 263-2800

Web site: http://www.cbcfinc.org

The Congressional Black Caucus Foundation is an organization of African American members of Congress dedicated to the cause of human and civil rights for all citizens.

DuSable Museum of African American History

740 East 74th Place

Chicago, IL 60639

(773) 947-0600

Web site: http://www.dusablemuseum.org

The DuSable Museum of African American History is the oldest museum in the country dedicated to the preservation and interpretation of African American history and culture.

U.S. Capitol

Capitol Building

Washington, DC 20515

(202) 226-2000

Web site: http://www.aoc.gov

The Capitol is home to the U.S. House of Representatives and the U.S. Senate.

White House

1600 Pennsylvania Avenue NW

Washington, DC 20500

(202) 456-2121

Web site: http://www.whitehouse.gov
The White House is the official home of the president of the
United States.

Web Sites

Due to the changing nature of Internet links, Rosen
Publishing has developed an online list of Web sites
related to the subject of this book. This site is updated
regularly. Please use this link to access the list:

http://www.rosenlinks.com/itn/elect

For Further Reading

Bausum, Ann. *Our Country's Presidents: All You Need to Know About the Presidents, from George Washington to Barack Obama*. Washington, DC: National Geographic, 2009.

Boyd, Herb. *We Shall Overcome*. Naperville, IL: Sourcebooks, Inc., 2004.

Colbert, David. *Michelle Obama: An American Story*. New York, NY: Houghton Mifflin Harcourt, 2009.

Gormley, Beatrice. *Barack Obama: Our 44th President*. New York, NY: Aladdin Paperbacks, 2008.

Ingram, Scott. *The 1963 Civil Rights March*. Milwaukee, WI: World Almanac Library, 2005.

Karson, Jill, ed. *The Civil Rights Movement*. Farmington Hills, MI: Greenhaven Press, 2005.

McKissack Jr., Frederick L. *This Generation of Americans: A Story of the Civil Rights Movement*. Columbus, OH: Waterbird Books, 2004.

Sharp, Anne Wallace. *A Dream Deferred: The Jim Crow Era*. Farmington Hills, MI: Lucent Books, 2005.

Taylor, Mildred B. *Roll of Thunder, Hear My Cry*. New York, NY: Dial Press, 1976.

Bibliography

Associated Press. "Obama Backs Off Holder's Race Comment." MSNBC.com, March 7, 2009. Retrieved April 30, 2009 (http://www.msnbc.msn.com/id/29571571).

Bumiller, Elisabeth. "McCain Parries a Reprise of 2000 Smear Tactics." *New York Times*, January 17, 2008. Retrieved April 30, 2009 (http://www.nytimes.com/2008/01/17/us/politics/17carolina.html).

Gerstile, Gary. *American Crucible: Race and Nation in the Twentieth Century*. Princeton, NJ: Princeton University Press, 2001.

Ifill, Gwen. *The Breakthrough: Politics and Race in the Age of Obama*. New York, NY: Doubleday, 2009.

Ignatius, Adi, ed. *President Obama: The Path to the White House*. New York, NY: TIME Books, 2008.

Langer, Gary, et al. "Exit Polls: Storm of Voter Dissatisfaction Lifts Obama to an Historic Win." ABC News, November 5, 2008. Retrieved April 30, 2009 (http://abcnews.go.com/PollingUnit/Vote2008/Story?id=6189129&page=1).

Meacham, Jon, ed. "How He Did It 2008." *Newsweek*, November 17, 2008.

Mendell, David. *Obama: From Promise to Power*. New York, NY: Amistad, 2007.

Obama, Barack. *The Audacity of Hope: Thoughts on Reclaiming the American Dream*. New York, NY: Three Rivers Press, 2006.

Obama, Barack. *Dreams from My Father: A Story of Race and Inheritance*. New York, NY: Random House, 1995.

Rogak, Lisa, ed. *Barack Obama in His Own Words: The Candidate Speaks on Everything from Abortion to the Middle East*. New York, NY: Carroll & Graf Publishers, 2007.

Shipler, David K. *A Country of Strangers: Blacks and Whites in America*. New York, NY: Vintage Books, 1997.

Steele, Shelby. *A Bound Man: Why We Are Excited About Obama and Why He Can't Win*. New York, NY: Fine Press, 2008.

Stolberg, Sheryl Gay, and Marjorie Connelly. "Obama Is Nudging Views on Race, a Survey Finds." *New York Times*, April 27, 2009. Retrieved April 30, 2009 (http://www.nytimes.com/2009/04/28/us/politics/28poll.html?_r=1).

Thomas, Evan, and *Newsweek*. *A Long Time Coming: The Inspiring, Combative 2008 Campaign and the Historic Election of Barack Obama*. New York, NY: PublicAffairs, 2009.

Wilson, John K. *Barack Obama: This Improbable Quest*. Boulder, CO: Paradigm Publishers, 2008.

Index

P
Palin, Sarah, 50
Powell, Colin, 23–24

R
race relations, U.S., 6–10, 14–17, 55
Rush, Bobby, 29–30

S
segregation, 7, 14, 15, 22
slavery, tragedy of, 8–10, 55

U
U.S. Census, 6
U.S. Secret Service, 39

V
Voting Rights Act of 1965, 7, 15

W
Wilder, L. Douglas, 11, 22–23, 32, 40–41
Wright, Jeremiah, 42–43, 46, 49

About the Author

Jason Porterfield is a journalist and writer living in Chicago, Illinois. He graduated from Oberlin College, where he majored in English, history, and religion. He has written more than twenty books for Rosen Publishing, including several covering historical subjects such as the Lincoln-Douglas debates and the early history of the Democratic Party.

Photo Credits

Cover (top, left) Mark Ralston/AFP/Getty Images; cover (top, right) Bob Parent/Hulton Archive/Getty Images; cover (bottom), p. 35 Scott Olson/Getty Images; pp. 4, 9, 12, 18 Library of Congress Prints and Photographs Division; p. 5 Timothy A. Clary/AFP/Getty Images; p. 21 Stan Honda/AFP/Getty Images; pp. 16, 28, 31, 33, 54 © AP Images; pp. 14, 24 Diana Walker/Time & Life Pictures/Getty Images; p. 26 Joe Raedle/Getty Images; pp. 34, 43 Brian Baer-Pool/Getty Images; p. 38 William Thomas Cain/Getty Images; pp. 44, 50 Chris Hondros/Getty Images; p. 45 Charles Ommanney/Getty Images; p. 47 Tony Karumba/AFP/Getty Images; pp. 51, 52 Jonathan Torgovnik/Getty Images.

Designer: Tom Forget; Photo Researcher: Amy Feinberg